TALES of MADISON FAITH

BUTTON, Buckle, Tie.

By Kim MacGregor

Illustrations by Sharon Snider & Todd Reny

with a special message from Céline Dion

Other Tales of Madison Faith Books:

"Yummy Yummy Nummy Nummy, should I put this in my tummy?
To find out more about Madison Faith and the people behind this series
Visit us at: www.talesofmadisonfaith.com

What People are saying about Tales of Madison Faith books:

"An Author who truly understands a child's mind has written a story that invites participation. All the elements of a fun story - **Yummy Yummy** is silly and predictable. A book which could be shared and enjoyed by children of all ages and those who have lived with a toddler.... truly delectable !"

L. Dodwell - JK/SK Kindergarten teacher Silverthorn Junior School

"My daughter Laura and I enjoyed your book immensely, it did not take long for her to learn the little rhyme "**Yummy Yummy Nummy Nummy** .... can't wait for the next one."   R. De Lorenzi, Toronto

"**Yummy Yummy**, is charming and delightful. The story is as adorable as the illustrated Madison. We are looking forward to reading this over and over. Thank you for writing our newest and lovely kids book."

A. Fritsch, Chicago, IL

Special thanks to the following kind souls:

Sharon and Todd for ALL their dedication and partnership
Céline Dion for her wonderful support of CCFF
The Canadian Cystic Fibrosis Foundation for successful/promising research
The Kinsmen and Kinnette Clubs of Canada for all their CF fundraising efforts
Benjamin Koo for ALL of his patience

Text copyright © 2003 by Kim MacGregor
Illustrations copyright © 2003 by Sharon Snider and Todd Reny
All rights reserved

No part of this work covered by the copyrights heron
may be reproduced or used in any form or by any means -
graphic, electronic, or mechanical - without the prior
written permission of the publisher.

Published in Canada by Beautiful Beginnings Youth Inc.
60-8 Bristol Road East, Suite 102 Mississauga, Ontario L4Z 3K8
Send us your thoughts/comments by e-mail at: macgregor3@idirect.com

Printed and bound in Hong Kong, China by Book Art Inc., Toronto
1 2 3 4 5 6   07 06 05 04 03

National Library of Canada Cataloguing in Publication
MacGregor, Kim, 1968-
Button, buckle, tie / Kim MacGregor ; illustrators,
Sharon Snider and Todd Reny.

(Tales of Madison Faith, ; v.1, no. 2)
Poems.
ISBN 0-9731301-4-8 (bound).--ISBN 0-9731301-3-X (pbk.)

1. Clothing and dress--Juvenile poetry. 2. Children's
poetry, Canadian (English). I. Snider, Sharon, 1951- II. Reny,
Todd, 1972- III. Title. IV. Series: MacGregor, Kim, 1968-
Tales of Madison Faith ; v. 1, no. 2.

PS8575.G825B88 2003   jC811'.6   C2003-903238-8
PZ7

TALES *of* MADISON FAITH

For my brother JR who taught me how to "buckle" down in life
and live with HOPE. - KM

For Mom and Dad who taught me to button, buckle, tie and a whole lot more. - SS

For Georgia and our "little one" who have me tied around their little fingers. - TR

" I am delighted that a portion of the proceeds from this wonderful series of
storybooks will be donated to the Canadian Cystic Fibrosis Foundation. Kim
MacGregor and I have two things in common; we are both mothers, and cystic
fibrosis has touched both of our families. I lost my beloved niece Karine to CF in
1993. I have long been a supporter of the Canadian Cystic Fibrosis Foundation
and its efforts to find a cure for this devastating disease. Kim's contribution
to this effort is truly admirable."

Céline Dion, Celebrity Patron of the
Canadian Cystic Fibrosis Foundation

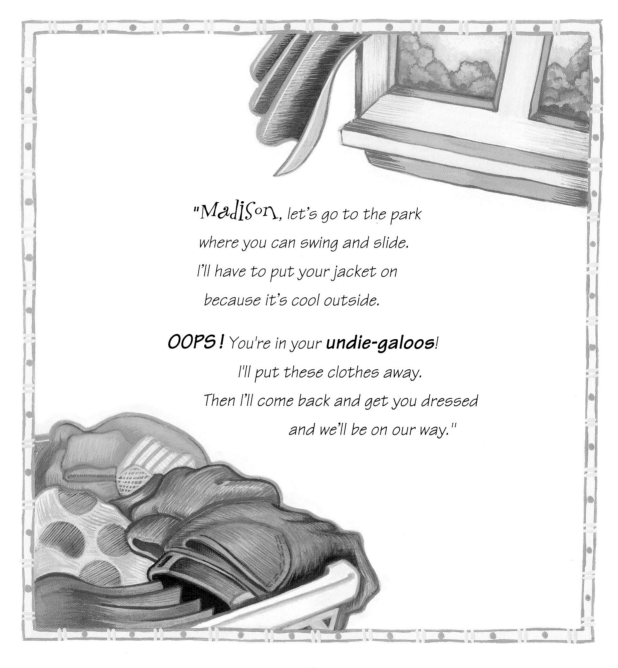

"Madison, let's go to the park
where you can swing and slide.
I'll have to put your jacket on
because it's cool outside.

OOPS! You're in your **undie-galoos**!
I'll put these clothes away.
Then I'll come back and get you dressed
and we'll be on our way."

I'll dress **myself** while Mom is gone,
she won't believe her eyes.
First I'll put my jacket on,
Mom sure will be surprised!

ONE, Two, Zippety-doo!

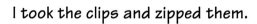

I took the clips and zipped them.

WOW!

I am so BIG and GROWN!

I did it up! I zipped it up!

I did it on my own!

And now I pick my shirt and pants,

my belt and running shoes.

I open up the drawer and then

I get my socks in twos.

It's **FUN** to get dressed by myself
but I just have to say,
if I'm to wear these clothes outside
there's lots to learn today.

Like how to **BUTTON** buttons and
how my belt should **buckle**.

And how to **tie** my running shoes
— don't want to trip in muckle.

I think that you can help me out,
just tell me what to do.
Should I **buckle** up my **new** shirt?
And **buckle** my belt too?

Should I **BUTTON** up my laces?
Or **tie** them up with glue?
Can you give me a little help?
And tell me what to do?

I'll start with my new **stripy** shirt,
it has two sides to match.
One side has lots of tiny holes,
one side has balls to catch,

I know the shirt joins at the top
and also in the middle.
Do I push each ball through each hole
with a **little fiddle twiddle**?

Say it! Yell it! Shout it out!
Please tell me what to try.
Should I **BUTTON**, buckle, tie
-buckle-tie-tie-tie?

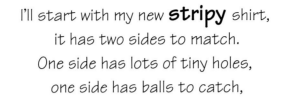

BUTTON!

Next I count four loops that loop
the whole way round my pants.
My checkered belt goes underneath
just like a limbo dance.

My belt has holes, a buckle and
one small bit with a wobble.
Do I push the bit through each hole
with a **bobble dobble hobble**?

Say it! Yell it! Shout it out!
Please tell me what to try.
Should I **BUTTON**, buckle, tie
-buckle-tie-tie-tie?

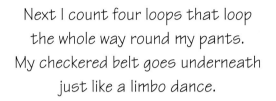

buckle !

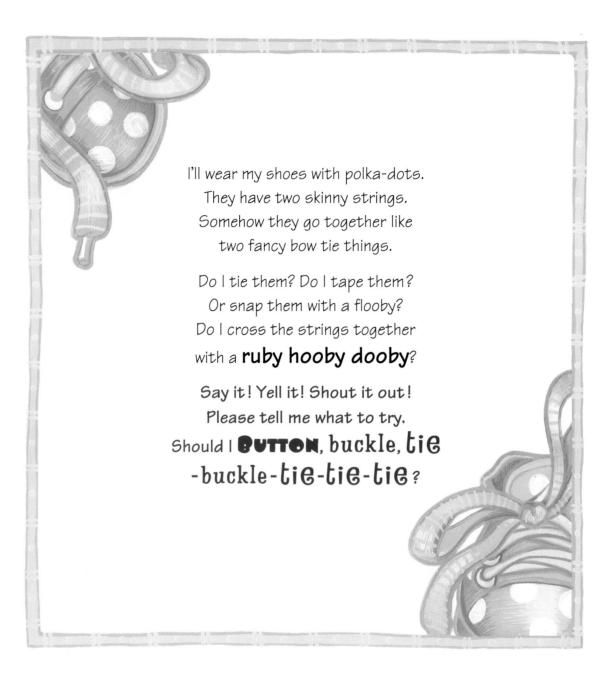

I'll wear my shoes with polka-dots.
They have two skinny strings.
Somehow they go together like
two fancy bow tie things.

Do I tie them? Do I tape them?
Or snap them with a flooby?
Do I cross the strings together
with a **ruby hooby dooby**?

Say it! Yell it! Shout it out!
Please tell me what to try.
Should I **BUTTON**, buckle, tie
-buckle-tie-tie-tie?

A hat with hearts and sunglasses,
(I'm almost fully dressed).
Add Mom's necklace, with a knapsack
and Grandma's hand-knit vest.

Ta-da, Voila, Oohh -la-la!

I'm so fancy me-oh-my!
Surprise, Mom! Look what I've done!
A **BUTTON**-buckle-tie!

I'm in colored stripes and checkers,
pink hearts and polka dots.
Clothes that **BUTTON**, shoes that tie
and Mom's necklace with spots.

Thank-you for helping me get dressed.
It sure was lots of **FUN**!
Now I'm off to the park with Mom,
I really have to run.

BUTTON, buckle, tie.
Buckle-tie-tie-tie!
BUTTON, buckle, tie.
Adios, bye-bye!